William Carey Richards

Thanksgiving for peace

A sermon, preached in the First Congregational church

William Carey Richards

Thanksgiving for peace
A sermon, preached in the First Congregational church

ISBN/EAN: 9783337224707

Printed in Europe, USA, Canada, Australia, Japan

Cover: Foto ©Lupo / pixelio.de

More available books at **www.hansebooks.com**

THA

PREAC

NAT

YORK :

& COMPANY,

ROADWAY.

866.

THANKSGIVING FOR PEACE;

A SERMON,

PREACHED IN THE FIRST CONGREGATIONAL CHURCH, AT
PITTSFIELD, MASS., ON THE OCCASION OF THE

NATIONAL AND STATE THANKSGIVING;

DECEMBER 7, 1865,

BY

WILLIAM C. RICHARDS,

PASTOR OF THE BAPTIST CHURCH, PITTSFIELD.

———

" Victoria concordia crescit."

———

NEW YORK :
SHELDON & COMPANY,
498 BROADWAY.
1866.

CORRESPONDENCE.

PITTSFIELD, Dec. 10, 1865.

Rev. Prof. RICHARDS,

Very dear Sir : —We, the undersigned, who heard your "National Thanksgiving Sermon," on the 7th instant, were so impressed with its liberal and conservative spirit, as to earnestly desire that it may be given to the people in some permanent form.

We therefore respectfully request a copy for publication.

THOMAS COLT,	H. M. PEIRSON,
GEO. P. BRIGGS,	M. H. WOOD,
W. R. PLUNKETT,	J. D. FRANCIS,
W. B. RICE,	C. V. SPEAR,
J. L. PECK,	E. S. FRANCIS,
E. B. WILSON,	L. G. BURNELL,

PITTSFIELD, Dec. 15, 1865.

GENTLEMEN :

It cannot be otherwise than gratifying to me to know that my views and utterances in my Thanksgiving Sermon, commend themselves to your cordial approbation. With the hope that their extension beyond the immediate audience to which they were spoken, will contribute a little to the great wo . of making the Peace which God has given us, an equal blessing to the North and the South, I cheerfully comply with your request, and remain,

Very truly yours,

WM. C. RICHARDS.

Messrs. THOS. COLT, GEO. P. BRIGGS, and others.

A PROCLAMATION.

Whereas, It has pleased Almighty God, during the year which is now coming to an end, to relieve our beloved country from the fearful scourge of civil war, and permit us to secure the blessings of peace, unity and harmony, with a great enlargement of civil liberty ;

And whereas, Our Heavenly Father has also, during the year, graciously averted from us the calamities of foreign war, pestilence and famine, while our granaries are all full of the fruits of an abundant season ;

And whereas, a righteousness exalteth a Nation, while sin is a reproach to any people :

Now, therefore, I, ANDREW JOHNSON, President of the United States, do hereby recommend to the people thereof that they do set apart and observe the first Thursday of December as a day of Thanksgiving to the Creator of the Universe, for their deliverance and blessings.

And I do further recommend that, on that occasion, the whole people make confession of our National sins against his Infinite goodness, and with one heart and one mind implore the Divine guidance in the ways of National virtue and holiness.

In testimony whereof, I have hereunto set my hand and caused the seal of the United States to be affixed.

Done at the City of Washington, this twentieth day of October,

[L. S.]   in the year of our Lord one thousand eight hundred and sixty-five, and of the Independence of the United States the ninetieth.

(Signed,)   ANDREW JOHNSON.

THANKSGIVING FOR PEACE.

"O come, let us sing unto the Lord ; let us make a joyful noise to the Rock of our Salvation.

"Let us come before His presence with thanksgiving,
and make a joyful noise unto Him with psalms."

PSALMS XCV. 1, 2.

THE sacred challenge of the inspired Psalm-
ist comes to us to-day in a double echo. We
are assembled in this sanctuary in obedience
to two proclamations ; one from the Gov-
ernor of our Commonwealth, and another
from the Chief Magistrate of the Republic ;
both of which call us, as the summons of the
Royal Poet called his people of old, to the
service and sacrifice of Thanksgiving unto
God.

Our State Thanksgiving which has hitherto
concentrated, in its almost immemorial fes-

tival, the quickest and profoundest emotions
of our hearts—and which has exalted itself
from a custom into almost the sanctity of a
sacred ordinance—is, to-day, blended with a
National service, of such peculiar dignity,
and of such irresistible force of fitness, that,
in effect, the former is merged and absorbed
into the latter. We keep indeed both festivals at once, and while fealty to the Commonwealth, and fidelity to the principles be-
queathed to us by our fathers, forbid us to
omit the State ordinance, we yet joyfully
consent to overlay its gifts upon the altar
with the broader and more special offerings
of gratitude and praise, due from us as an
integral part of the great Nation coming up,
to-day, with Thanksgiving to the Lord.

Five years have passed away since any
State of the American Union celebrated its
annual Thanksgiving, in such circumstances
of peace and prosperity, as would naturally

inspire the song of praise upon our lips and melody in our hearts unto God. Four times our own Commonwealth has been summoned to this service, while the clouds of calamity hung thickly in the national sky ; and while upon all the horizon there was scarcely a ray of light to be seen. The din of battle, the shock of arms, the "confused noise and garments rolled in blood," the slaughter of our brothers and sons, and innumerable other tokens of the melancholy prevalence of civil war within our borders—seemed almost mockeries of our successive festivals, making of them, to multitudes, times of fasting rather than of feasting ; occasions for sorrow rather than of song ; and clouding them, even to the most favoured and hopeful participant, with the shadows of impenetrable gloom.

I cannot but remember and recall here, the emotions with which, in a sister and contiguous State, I prepared to obey the call of its

Executive for public Thanksgiving services four years ago. Then the first fearful surprise—the awe I may fitly say—of the National calamity was upon all hearts. There was a paralysis of almost every arm of wonted industry. Looms were idle. The wings of commerce were folded. The strokes of labour fell feebly and with many intermissions. The only activities were of a strange and startling nature. They were the activities of vast and augmenting preparations for war. The foundry and the forge were aglow with the lurid fires that melted and moulded the iron for Death's deadly implements.

In these circumstances, the Thanksgiving proclamation of 1861, in our New England States, and doubtless in others, had, at first, a tone of untimeliness in it. Some asked with irony, some with bitterness, some with only heedlessness—" What have we to be thankful for ?" Without misgiving, I charged my peo-

ple. in the words of Nehemiah, "Go your
way; eat the fat—drink the sweet, and send
portions unto them for whom nothing is prepared. For this day is holy unto our God :
Neither be ye sorry, for the joy of the Lord is
your strength."* There were darker clouds
upon the national sky, on subsequent Thanksgiving days, than those which infolded the
annual feast in 1861. But we had become
too familiar with their gloom to fear them as
we did at first. And having risen once to
the grandeur of the occasion, and offered unto
God Thanksgiving in War; remembering
His mercies in the midst of judgments ; look-
ing through the lurid smoke of battle upon
plentiful harvests ; hearing, in the intervals
of the sullen boom of the cannon, the sweet
tones of Divine promise—"For a small moment have I forsaken thee ; but with great

* Nehemiah viii, 10.

2

mercies will I gather thee ;"* we were encouraged and strengthened to meet every recurrence of the festival with renewed confidence in the final success of our cause and in the restored favour of Heaven.

And this day, my hearers, we hold the Thanksgiving for Peace. *Peace* is the foremost blessing, of that throng of Divine gifts, for which we come, to-day, " before His presence with Thanksgiving, and make a joyful noise unto Him with psalms."

With a noble fitness our Chief Magistrate calls upon the Nation to thank God for *Peace.* I am glad that he did not substitute for this sweet, this significant, this pregnant, this all-embracing word—that other word—which perhaps a less thoughtful, less gentle, less catholic mind would have seized upon as the watchword of the great National Thanksgiving

* Isaiah, liv, 7.

summons : I mean the word *Victory*. I say,
I am glad the President did not substitute
Victory for *Peace* in his proclamation. He
might have done this and our beautiful flag,
with its stars and stripes everywhere waving
in the breeze, would have justified the word.
The dispersion of the rebel armies ; the hu-
miliation of their proud and skillful leaders ;
the surrender of their strongholds ; the ur-
gency of their chief men in their pleas for the
Executive Pardon ; the restoration of Federal
authority in courts and citadels, recently
proud and defiant with Rebellion ; these and
a thousand other signs would have warranted
the use of the word. Why, then, am I glad
it was not used ? Because the Victory which
has been achieved is more *worthily* expressed,
and, indeed, only fitly expressed in the sweet
word Peace. Had we not conquered a Peace,
we had won no Victory. If the Roman people held, as we are told by the historian, and

without the influence of christianity, that
there *could be no victories in civil war*—how
much more shall we, under the moulding
power of the gospel, hold that every victory
of arms we obtained over our rebellious bre-
thren was yet but our melancholy defeat, as
much as theirs, until we had subdued their
hearts.

For our sectional victories over their sectional revolt; for our arms triumphant over
their weapons; it had been mockery—and
the refinement of it—for the representative
of our still undivided Nation to call them
with us to *Thanksgiving.* His call is not to
Massachusetts in her proud loyalty, any more
than to South Carolina in her bitter repent-
ance; but to both alike and together; at the
common altar of National sacrifice, to give
thanks unto Him, whose arm hath gotten Him
the Victory—not for Massachusetts and not
over Carolina; but for them both as parts of

the great and undissevered league of States, that but yesterday seemed about to be dissolved in blood ; but, to-day, is by that very blood—a solvent no more, but a cement—compacted into a unity before impracticable.

Had the call been to Thanksgiving for Victory, instead of Peace, how sadly marred would not the people's compliance with it have appeared ! At first we think, perhaps, that there could have been no imperfection, no dimness on the glory of New England's votive offerings unto God at this hour. She had sighed and longed and prayed and toiled and sacrificed and bled *for Victory*. While the Rebellion was erect and defiant and insolent, the thirst for victory, for the red trophy of conquest, for the humbling of a proud foe, for the degradation of a false standard and a usurping banner, for the retributive punishment of the begettors and abettors of Treason —the thirst for these things, though in a

sense sanguinary, did not seem to be alto-
gether unreasonable. Yet, had it been, the
real and not the seeming, the deep and not
the superficial sentiment of the heart of New
England—had there been beneath it all no
profounder, no purer, no more patriotic and
philanthropic purpose and prayer—we must
have been convicted, my hearers, of putting
an estimate on triumphs in civil strife which
the unchristian public sentiment of Rome
scorned. But even New England--the blood
of so many of whose gallant sons has reddened
the soil, and tinged the streams of Southern
battle fields—would not have given thanks to
God, to-day, for mere physical victories,
however many or magnificent they might
have been ; if dominant in all, and over all
the sounds of loyal victory, there were not,
swelling upon every breeze, and echoing from
the beetling cliffs of ocean, and the bluffs of
mighty rivers, North, South, East and West,

the heavenly pæans of Peace. It is for Peace, and not for Victory, that the heart of New England is thankful to-day. The mother whose noble boy fell in the battle ; the grey-haired sire who has no son left to take his place, because his country needed him for a sacrifice ; even these are breathing out of their swelling, sobbing bosoms, not the fiery, feverish word Victory, but the sweet, sooth-ing, healing word—Peace !

But if even in our loyal States, a thanks-giving for mere *Victory* must have been a blemished and distorted offering—as savour-ing to multitudes of the spirit of Moloch and not of the Messiah—what shall I say of the hollow mockeries of compliance with the Thanksgiving call, which would be now enacting solemn falsehoods and sacred farces in the sanctuaries of the people who were, but a few months ago, englamoured with the spells of Secession and the hope of successful

Revolution ! Where, in all the region over which the flag of revolt waved, would a Thanksgiving for Victory—I mean for the triumph of Northern over Southern force— have been anything but a lie ? For would it not have been the exultation of the vanquished over their defeat; their rejoicing in what their pride must count as their shame ! There could have been no Thanksgiving, to-day, in Virginia, in Carolina, in Georgia— amid the ruins of desolated towns, the blackened skeletons of once fair forests, the ravaged fields where always plenty smiled, the wrecks of a luxurious prosperity, and the still present signs of the conqueror's power and authority. It needed that the form of Victory should be disguised at least, with the beautiful habiliments of *Peace*, in order that the subdued and yet spirited sons of the South should come to the festival of the Nation with any other aspect and spirit than that of sul-

lenness and shame. And, my hearers, if there
is not more in the national heart and inten-
tion, than a mere disguising of Victory's
proud form in the lovely vestments of Peace ;
if the substitution is seeming and not *real*,
there will be still victory, perhaps, but not,
in perpetuity, that which makes victory of
value—amity, brotherhood, charity !

Thanksgiving for Peace ! This is the re-
quisition ; this the sweet, welcome, easy duty
of the day and the hour. It excludes no part
of the regenerated and delivered land ; no
State of all the great family so recently
plunged in the wild turmoil and turbulence
of a strife, which, for deadly earnestness and
deadly peril to both parties, had never a
parallel in history. Before the blessed image
of Peace which has been set up at the National
Capital, there is no reason why every lately
revolted State shall not come and, with every
other loyal State, cast down its pledge of

fidelity and lift up its song of Thanksgiving
to God.   In the Thanksgiving for *Peace* all
partizan wranglings may fitly be hushed.
Although months have elapsed since Peace
was virtually achieved—its public proclamation has waited for the utterance of National
Praise ; that the clamours of section and party
prejudice might have time to rage and swell
and diminish, until now they should utterly
die away, while the universal song of Thanksgiving soars heavenward from the National
heart.

Peace has returned to our land.   The grim
visage of war is shrinking into the shadows
of the past.   The soldier is laying aside his
arms and resuming the implements of industry.   The forge is taxed no longer, day and
night alike, with a demand for deadly weapons.   Already the spades which heaved the
soil into ominous billows of wrath, are level-
ling the mounds for the happy toil of the hus-

bandman. Arsenals are no longer the hope
of the country. Academies resume their as-
cendancy. Military tribunals yield up their
usurped functions to the civil courts, and the
scales of justice hang no longer from the
glittering, but unstable sword-hilt. Forts, if
not dismantled—as prudence disallows—
swarm no longer with crowded garrisons.
Battle-ships are transformed into merchant-
men. Our great railways are blocked no
longer with troops and munitions of War;
but rapidly exchange the generous produce
of the teeming fields and prairies of the West,
for the ingenious and useful products of the
busy looms and workshops of the East.

The familiarity of the National mind with
wholesale carnage and havoc is receding into
that natural and wholesome horror of blood,
from which it was violently dragged forth by
fierce battles and slaughters, whose distinc-
tive names are burdensome, for their multi-

tude, to the memory. Everything around us speaks the promise of a National prosperity, which may have simulations, indeed, in a time of War, but can be substantial only in a time of Peace.

If to us of the loyal States, never impoverished by the progress of the War, but on the contrary displaying, in the face of a gigantic Terror—threatening our political and social ruin, a constantly recuperative energy, amazing to the nations of Europe and hardly less so to ourselves ; if to us, upon whom the dread burden of War has pressed with comparatively little force, the advent of Peace with all her attendant train of blessings, is an occasion for ardent thanksgiving—how can it be less to the people whom the War has reduced from a proud affluence to almost penury, and who have seen—in the track of the unhindered march of an avenging Government—not only their estates despoiled, their possessions consumed, their strength wasted, their armies overwhelmed, but beyond these disasters—their cherished institutions and ideas shattered and dissipated in the tempest, until they rest from a hopeless conflict enfeebled and indeed exhausted. Must not Peace be welcome to them? They might indeed scorn it at the hands of an alien foe, though his foot were upon their necks! We should expect this from those in whose veins our blood courses, and whom we could not afford to despise in the field. But at the hands of the Nation, of which they and we are equally integers, why should they not take the beautiful olive branch, already blossomed thickly with the signs of happier days, and press it to their wan lips with fervent praises to God!

For Peace shall be even more to them than to us—if heartily embraced and thoroughly appreciated. To us it will bring renewed

3

and, it may be, augmented prosperity. To them it will be not a progress only, but a new birth ; not an enhancement of good alone, but a new inheritance. Under the sway of the new Angel of Peace—the social life, the political condition, the industrial resources, the very soil of the beautiful and generous southern clime will find regeneration and bourgeon into aspects and products of beauty and wealth, which we of this less genial clime may yet, with brotherly kindness come to envy.

But I shall disappoint your just expectations, and do injustice to this great National occasion for Thanksgiving, if I find no other reason for it than the restoration of Peace.

There are, indeed, two other grounds upon which, if the service we render to-day needed to be justified, I should confidently stand up for its vindication. At one of these I shall merely glance—assured that the briefest ob-

servation of it will suffice to convince you
that it is solid and no quicksand; no deceit-
ful mirage merely.

Our gratitude, as a Nation, is due to Him
who holds the destiny of kingdoms and dy-
nasties in His hand, for *the preservation of
this Union of States without a flaw.* The
disintegration of the Union, to the extent con-
templated and so vehemently desired by the
States recently in revolt, would have been a
calamity, the measure of which we shall now
never determine; but which might, perhaps,
have been unfolded, to the loyal and dis-
loyal alike, in the endurance of the inevitable
political, social and personal misfortunes
which would have been the only fruits of our
National dismemberment. In some sense, I
know, these alleged woes are only conjec-
tural, but I have, again and again, sought to
look with strained eyes into the thick gloom
of Disunion, if haply I might discover there

some faint promise of good to both, or even
to one, of the great divorced parties. While
I did not, indeed, desire to find some such
sign, I think there were times, in the gloomy
and weary march of events, when it would
have given me some sort of comfort to say to
my burdened heart—"Well poor, troubled
heart, if the worst comes to the worst, and
this glorious league of married States is broken in violent divorcement—there is yet a
gleam, a ray perhaps, of promise on the far
horizon, that may grow into brightness for
the divided peoples." But I could not dis-
cern that gleam. All beyond the melancholy
disruption was dark with the presage and
presence of disorder and strife. I saw not
then, any more than I see now, how States
drifted asunder by conflicting principles and
policies—till the fierce strain snapped the
cable that held them together, should there-
after peacefully and prosperously sail in the

same sea, the jurisdiction of whose waters
and shores must be forever in perplexing
question, and often in complications of doubt,
ending only in fierce and bitter and relentless
antagonisms and strifes—hindering progress
and imperilling the existence of one or both.
With the imminence of the *danger* connected
with the disjunction of the States—a danger
circumscribed, to the deliberate judgment of
multitudes, by no narrower sweep than the
wild orbit of anarchy—the violence such a
catastrophe would do to the patriotism and
affection with which loyal hearts cherished
the Union, devised by the wisdom, framed by
the toil and cemented by the blood of our
fathers, was as nothing, in comparison, while
yet the result was impending as a fearful pos-
sibility of doom; but now that the doom is
averted, by the Divine interposition, we feel,
in all its absolute terribleness, the anguish it
would have cost us to see the beautiful fabric

of American popular government crumbled into fragments, by the fratricidal strength of those to whom its pillars should have been more dear than their personal aggrandizement, more sacred than their fondest ambitions. Shuddering, as we must, to realize the extreme narrowness of our escape from ruin, with the overthrow of our National temple, we recover our calmness only before the altar of Him, whose wisdom and strength and grace constituted the trinity of force required for the conservation of a Government too exceptional and too beneficent, in the history of nations, to be jeopardized by caprice, or ambition, without the deep dishonour of those who dared the crime, and without our grateful acknowledgments to Him who prevented its dread consummation.

The third reason I shall offer for our hearty observance of this service of gratitude to God is *the extension and perfection of our National*

Liberty. I use the word perfection in a relative rather than in an absolute sense, and as applied to the scope, rather than to the quality of freedom resulting from the great convulsions of the Union. Without conviction— without even the thought—that the extinction of American slavery, existing as it did by the suffrage of the great Charter of our Federal organization, would have been a wise and worthy end of an internecine war ; or, in its bare accomplishment, a vindication of the measures in which such a war had its origin on the part of the Government ; I am nevertheless not only prepared, but profoundly eager, to " make a joyful noise unto the Rock of our Salvation," for the result of Emancipation, as incidental to the progress of the conflict betwixt unconditional loyalty to the. Union, and uncompromising hostility to it. The logic of events is too resistless to be opposed with mere preferences of judgment as to the manner in which truly grand and immeasurably lofty moral consummations shall be reached.

The uprooting of Slavery was of this order of consummations, 'devoutly to be wished'; and in the face of its astonishing achievement, all merely judicial scruples as to the doing of it assume the aspect of solemn impertinence. The ship with the dark flag has gone down in the tempest madly evoked for its preservation from a form of ruin, which existed, perhaps, only in the imagination of those whose idolatry of it disturbed their reason. They counted its perpetuation as more to be desired than the conservation of the Government, which yet held in its Charter all the warrants it could boast, or claim, for its continuance; and in their reckless zeal to immolate the Constitution of the United States, they brought Slavery, instead, within the sacrificial stroke of the knife and the fire. And

now over its blood and its consuming corpse,
how shall the Nation do less than rejoice with
trembling, and give unfeigned thanks to God
for His salvation vouchsafed to us, from the
peril of a fearful cancer in the body politic—
which, disguised as it might be, was never
stripped of its terror, and yet was in such
close proximity to the life of the Nation, that
no hand but God's could ply the knife and
cut the festering death away.

I am claiming—observe my hearers—that
the extension of Freedom to the enslaved race
in the midst of us, is a fit occasion for National
Thanksgiving to God. I do not now think
of sectional interests, but of universal interests. If I did not sincerely believe that the
people, upon whom the sacrifice of Slavery
has fallen with the immediate aspect of a
calamity, and who, from their long association
with it, and from their general unconscious-
ness, and inapprehension even, of any social

or moral wrong-doing in maintaining, defending and perpetuating it ; if I did not believe, I repeat, that the late slave-owners have fully as much reason as any of us—aye vastly more than any of us—and not less, by the least whit, than the emancipated slaves themselves, to give thanks to God for the very thing they shunned, as the worst of evils and the saddest of disasters, I should not think it possible for this Thanksgiving festival to be in any just and broad sense—National. Millions of the people of the United States would be unable to unite with other millions in the recognition of what these latter will doubtless most exult in to-day, as ground for National praises to our Fathers God—the emancipation of all the slaves in our land. But on this point I am in no perplexity of mind or conscience. The deliverance of the slave-holder is as great as that vouchsafed to the slave. Both are emancipated. The freedom of the slave is the freedom of the master. I can well appreciate the feeling with which one of the latter class, in Georgia, said to his father—also a slave-holder—the morning when the President's final decree of Emancipation was received, "I congratulate you, sir, that you and I are both freemen now." The father's perception was not so quick as that of his son, but it needed only the impulsion of the felicitous thought, seconded by a few words of explanation, and father and son shook hands and looked into one another's faces with smiles of unwonted brightness, as they felt together that, in Slavery's overthrow, they were enlarged. And while I cannot flatter myself, or you, with the idea that a majority of the late slave-masters of the South have reached the Pisgah of a vision, so broad and fair as at I have alluded to, I do believe that thousands are climbing to it, and that ere long the people of the South will atone for any lack

of fervour in their gratitude to-day for Emancipation, by originating a special Thanksgiving ordinance—for themselves, their children, and their children's children to honour.

The masters who held slaves were themselves slaves to the system of servitude and
its sad entail of evils upon the white class.
In the atmosphere of this unconscious servitude, Agriculture, Industrial Arts and Education were all dwarfed and stunted. Labour,
which is the vitality of a people, was dispar-
aged and dishonoured by Slavery. The slave
agriculture was slovenly and exhaustive to
the land. The childhood of the white class
was degraded, intellectually, by association
with the slave children. Without pressing
this view further, and without defining the
injustice of Slavery to the subjects of it, which
is foreign to my point, I insist that in an eco-
nomical and social—not to say *moral*—sense,
the extinction of Slavery will result speedily

to the vast benefit of those who may now sullenly, or more patiently, deplore the dispensation of Providence which has broken the yoke from the neck of the black man. A new industry, new processes of competitive agriculture, labour the law of the white man as well as of the black man, and compensation according to toil; these alone will prove grand and rapid regenerating forces in the now paralyzed and desolated South; and we shall see the wilderness blossom as the rose, and the people of that afflicted region will have appointed to them "beauty for ashes, the oil of joy for mourning, the garment of praise for the spirit of heaviness."

For this Jubilee Year then to the Southern land and its population, white and black alike, the National heart should pour out, to-day, its thankfulness to the Rock of our Salvation; the pulse and throb of the Southern heart answering to the pulse and throb of the North-

4

ern heart ; while the clanking of chains is a
sound dying away into the preludes of the
new song of universal liberty.

I do not forget, to-day, because I fail spe-
cially to dwell upon them, those reasons for
profound gratitude to Almighty God, which
are, from their constant recurrence, *not* extra-
ordinary, like those I have indicated. The
common blessings vouchsafed to us in the al-
ternation of the seasons, with their healthful
work and happy wages for it, with their out
of door charms and their home delights, are,
like ten thousand other gifts of our beneficent
and loving Father, the *staple* themes of our
thanksgiving. Surely, we are not less thankful for them, to-day, because they are for a
season overshadowed by the grander gifts
which make the year an *Annus Mirabilis* in
our National Annals. We look up now to
the great gift of Peace, as the pilgrim in the
Alps lifts his eye to the sky-piercing Matter-

horn ; its wondrous peak supplanting a little while all less, all lower objects in his regard. To that summit of our national elevation— which we call *Peace*, we lift *our* eyes to-day. We send our songs thitherward. We shout our anthems that the strain may soar and soar till that peak shall " catch the flying joy," and " roll the rapturous hosanna round."

This sermon would have an inexcusable imperfection in it (as I know it has other imperfections, which I trust in your generosity to hold excusable ;)—if I should close it without attempting to indicate some of the ways in which true thankfulness to God will reveal itself, not in the National voice alone, but in the National conduct.

The times are confessedly momentous. Every day may be shaping grand historical events. Every day is, indeed, maturing to perfect ripeness the fruit of the conflict ; or else hastening within its heart the melancholy

processes of blight and decay. And the people are individually responsible for the cha-
racter of National counsels and acts, mediately
if not immediately. It is, therefore, of vast
moment, that we should understand our re-
sponsibility, and with right judgment and
right action, acquit ourselves of it right man-
fully. The Peace and restored National Authority, and the wide extension of Freedom,
which are the experiences of the Nation, this
present memorable year, all demand the ex-
tremest wisdom for their conservation and
happiest development.

At the foundation of true National thankfulness to God, as the Rock of our Salvation.
lies, essentially, a profound sense of His interposition for us, in the fearful exigencies to
which we were brought by the Rebellion
and the War. Inseparable from such a con-
sciousness as this, is the conviction that only
the hand which saved us can keep us from

falling again and fatally. At such a doctrine as this Infidelity and Atheism may sneer. Rationalism may smile with ill-concealed scorn ; but spiritual Reason and Christian Faith, two divinely irradiated principles, which will endure when all the sneers and cavillings of unbelief shall be hushed in eternal silence, will accept and vitalize the doctrine into duty and obedience.

The speedy restoration of mutual confidence between the lately antagonistic sections of the Union is the pressing demand of the times. To effect this should be the aim of every enlightened statesman and of every true patriot. Upon the altar of true amity all partizan creeds and platforms and prejudices and schemes should be cast and consumed. The clamours of sectionalism should die away in fraternal words. In the accomplishment of a result so noble and lofty as this, the *initiative* clearly belongs to the successful

contestant in the now ended conflict. The
people, humiliated by defeat of every kind,
physical, political, social and moral ; smart-
ing with surprising hurts ; bewildered by
amazing revolutions ; confounded by the col-
lapse of bubbles which they fondly believed
were spheres of granite ; impoverished to a
degree of which their own serfs never afforded
an example, and their own generous land no
type ; awaking only with clouded and reluc-
tant eyes to the stern conviction that " old
things are passed away and all things are
made new " in their condition and destiny ;
distrusting and often utterly disbelieving the
professions of their successful competitors,
that they desire only the highest good of the
whole country—knowing no North and no
South ; dreaming yet, it may be, of impossi-
ble extrication from the meshes of Fate which
are about them ; the subdued, broken, disap-
pointed, discouraged, but yet generous, warm-

hearted, open-handed people of the lately
revolted regions, should be spared every
needless pang of fresh bitterness in the waters
of the full cup poured out to them. It is
ours, my hearers, it is Massachusetts' privilege to kill their lingering pride and hate and
doubt and defiance, with genuine magnanimity, with Christian kindness, with incontro-
vertible proofs that, Slavery being now mori-
bund and practically out of the way, there
is actually nothing between Massachusetts
and Carolina—as the representatives of all the
loyal and all the returning Commonwealths—
to hinder the true embrace of sisterly love
and fellowship.

The exercise of magnanimity is not within
the power of the South. This high privilege
belongs to the North. I do not mean that the
people of the South cannot be generous. I
mean only, that now they have nothing to
give but their consent to what being inevi-

table, they may allow with cheerfulness or
sullenness, with high resolves to make the
best of it, or stolid inaction as sufferers, according to the spirit and temper of those who
have the power of the majority to press what-
soever cup they will to the lips of the prone.

The people of the South can be won by
kindness. The people of the North can be
exalted, ennobled, enriched by the exercise
of kindness—than which God never ordained
an easier and happier method of a people's
aggrandizement. Henceforward, indeed, there
is but one people beneath the stars and the
stripes. The mad dream of another flag has
proved a baseless vision. The stars are not
for one section and the stripes for another ;
but both for all—the stars to multiply and
not the stripes.

We shall not be truly grateful to God
in this great epoch of deliverance, my hearers, if we do not hold our judgment and

our impulses in the strong leash of modera-
tion, while we discuss and determine the
grave matters originated by the new order of
things. We are unquestionably debtors to
the emancipated people of this country, to
the whole extent of the persistence and
vehemence with which we have desired their
freedom. A faithful discharge of our debt
to them will well attest the sincerity of our
gratitude to the Giver of Liberty. Our ef-
forts, our contributions, in their behalf, for
the amelioration of their sufferings in the
strange vicissitudes of sudden independence,
for their education, cultivation and conver-
sion, are all the legitimate sequences of our
hopes and prayers for their enlargement.

But even in this direction, there is need of
earnest and intelligent discrimination, lest
our impulses rush far beyond the limit of
judicious interference for them. The freedmen must, for obvious reasons, abide in the

South, either with or without the white class
which recently held them in Slavery. You
and I, and all thoughtful men, deprecate the
idea of a separate, isolated community of
colour. If, then, the white and coloured classes
are to dwell together, it is absolutely vain
for outside legislation to fix and define the
precise terms of their relationship. It is sa-
fer to entrust these grave questions to the
statesmanship and to the conscience of the
Southern people—who being obliged to ad-
just themselves to the new order of social
conditions, will not blindly override and op-
press those who must yet do their hard labour
for them. Moreover, I am persuaded that
there is a conscience in the South, which being now unbound from the green withs of an
almost irresponsible power over the slaves,
will rise up and assert itself in just require-
ments and judicious regulations for the
freedmen.

What we have to do at the North, is to co-operate with the yet crippled Southern people, in repairing the immeasurable damage they have sustained in their vain uprising against the Union, and by the gentleness of our spirit convince them of the true greatness of our social and political and moral status, that they may copy all its excellencies, and excel if they can, all the proudest developments of its worth and wisdom we have yet realized.

"Our whole country" is henceforth the true watchword of our lips and our hearts, and if we mean less than this to-day, our Thanksgiving must be marred. There will be discordant notes in its melody — which will gravitate it downward, instead of wafting it upward *to Heaven.*

Let us, my hearers, go forward, in our imagination, forward a whole decade—until we reach Thanksgiving Day in 1875. Some of

us will never see that day with other eyes
than those of imagination. Happy, I think,
will be those eyes that physically behold,
and those ears that physically hear, the scenes
and sounds of that not far distant day. If
the beneficent Father whom we worship, ac-
cepts the National service we bring, to-day,
to His altars—and He will accept it if we are
true patriots, true philanthropists and true
Christians,—then, upon this anniversary in
1875, there will stretch " from Eastern coast
to Western," a glorious league of *Forty married States*, the basis of whose magnificent
prosperity will be universal Liberty—under
the ægis of which no privileged class will op-
press or wrongfully restrain another class ;
but all will have their rights before the law
and before God. To all orders of the people,
to its forty millions of minds, the blessings
of Education will be accessible, and even ob-
trusive, so that " he who runs may read."

The great oceans, and the multitudinous seas and harbours of the world will be whitened with the sails of our commerce. The metals and the coals, from the mines and the measures of our great mineral storehouses, will help to vitalize and adorn the industry of all nations. The vast and fertile plains and prairies of the West and South will choke the granaries of Europe with food for its hungry masses, and tire her looms with staples for clothing her sons and daughters. Science, never idle, will have done in a decade of years, the marvels which before had no parallel in a decade of centuries. She will have reticulated the Western Continent with the iron web, every fibre of which is a filament of far reaching thought and speech. She will have linked the great seas together with bands of steel. She will have lighted our cities, our highways, our coasts, with carbon or metallic suns—almost literally fulfilling the inspired prediction, " For there is nothing

5

hid which shall not be manifested."* She
will have controlled the subtle and myste-
rious sisterhood of unseen forces—transform-
ing them into one another, and by their agency
combining the elements with a wondrous skill
for the benefit of man. All this will she
have done, and more : but most of all, she
will have revealed to us God, in earth and
sea and sky and air. God only wise, God only
great, God only to be worshipped with perpetual Thanksgiving.

On that Thanksgiving Day, if any of us,
my hearers, may not look forth upon the development I have imagined : may it be ours
to take part in a grander and loftier service
of Praise than will ever send its echoes flying
from spire to spire, from hill top to hill top,
on this round earth even in the perpetual
festival of Thanksgiving before the Throne of
God and the Lamb, in which all whom the Son
has made free by His blood, shall have part
" with joy unspeakable and full of glory."

*Mark iv. 22

www.ingramcontent.com/pod-product-compliance
Lightning Source LLC
Chambersburg PA
CBHW031823090426
42739CB00008B/1379